CCSS **Genre** Fiction

M000115070

? Essential Question
How can we protect Earth?

Family Night Unplugged

by Yolanda Garcia
illustrated by Michael Reid

CHAPTER 1

Earth Day

"Earth Day was so much fun today!" said Ben Rounds. Ben, his sister Courtney, and their friend Josh were heading home from school.

"It was super fun! What did you guys do in your classes?" Josh asked.

"A farmer came to our class," Courtney said. "He brought fruits and vegetables that he grew. He picked them this morning. You wouldn't believe how delicious they were!"

"Wow, lucky you," Ben said. "But we had fun, too. Our class took a trip to Simmons Park and played in this enormous tree with branches that hung down like a big tent. Then we got to walk over a path of stones that went across a stream. We saw fish swimming right by our feet! After we ate lunch, we partnered off and picked up trash around the park. We raced each other, so it was the greatest clean-up ever!"

3

"We're going on our field trip tomorrow," said Josh. "Today our class made bar graphs showing how much electricity different household objects use. I didn't know refrigerators used so much!"

"I wonder how much of the electric supply computers use," said Ben. "Hey, do you want to come to dinner tonight? My dad said he has a special Earth Day surprise planned!"

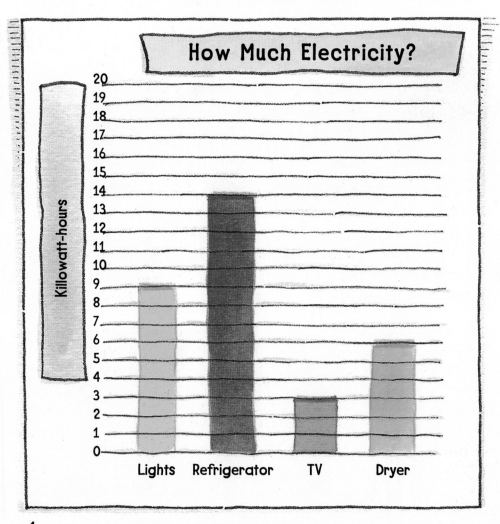

That night at dinner, Mr. Rounds made an announcement. "In honor of Earth Day, your mother and I have an unusual plan for tonight."

Courtney, Ben, and Josh were incredibly curious.

"We are going to turn out the lights and spend the whole evening without using any electricity!" said Mrs. Rounds.

"So we're going to sit in the dark? How boring!" Courtney groaned.

CHAPTER 2

Time to Unplug

"It will be fun, and I'm certain you can live for one night without electricity," Mr. Rounds said gently.

"We have some fantastic ideas," added Mrs. Rounds. "Don't worry; you'll see how much fun we can have while we're doing our part to save Earth."

The three children didn't say anything because they were trying to figure out a way to get out of the grown-ups' plan. "I'm not sure we really have a choice," whispered Courtney. Ben and Josh sighed.

They started out with a board game. "Good thing it's still light out," said Josh. "I mean, I wouldn't want you to miss any of my brilliant moves!" They all laughed and then groaned as they realized that Josh was ahead. The children barely noticed when Mrs. Rounds lit candles so they could see the board. Finally, the game was over, and Courtney was the surprise winner!

"Even if I hadn't won, I would have thought that was fun!" said Courtney proudly. "I wish we played games more instead of just watching TV."

The sun had set now, and it was dark but cozy. A streetlight gave the room a rosy glow.

"I know what you mean, Courtney," said Josh. "When I visit my grandparents' farm, we rarely turn on the TV. Instead, Grandma tells us stories about when she was a little girl. Things were so different then."

"That's really neat, Josh. I love to hear old stories, too," said Mr. Rounds. "My father always used to tell us stories about his camping trips. Grandpa was an expert at living with few Earth resources!"

"I remember the time we visited Grandma and Grandpa," said Courtney. "I thought it was a long distance to travel, but it was worth it!"

"Last time I was at my grandparents' farm, we ate carrots that came right out of the ground!" said Josh. "Until then, I never even thought about where our food comes from. I guess I just thought carrots grew in bags in the supermarket."

Courtney and Ben laughed. Even Mr. and Mrs. Rounds chuckled.

"Josh, can you show my mom and dad the graph you made today?" asked Ben.

"Sure!" replied Josh. He pulled out his graph and showed it to Mr. and Mrs. Rounds.

"I have an idea!" Josh exclaimed. "Let's go on a scavenger hunt around the house and make a list of things that use electricity. Next time we're at the library, we can research to find out how much each thing uses!"

They began making a list of each object that used electricity. Everyone agreed that the refrigerator probably used the most.

"I know what we can do that doesn't use electricity! Anyone know a good joke?" said Ben.

"I do," Courtney said. "Why was the baby ant so confused?" Nobody knew. "All of his uncles were ants!" laughed Courtney.

"That was a good one, Courtney. I have a joke, too," said Mom. "What do fish cheer at a football game?" Again, nobody knew. "GO FISH!" Mom said. The children looked puzzled. "Go Fish is a card game that we used to play when I was a kid," she explained. "Now that's another fun activity that doesn't use electricity."

"Well, I don't know about you guys, but I'm hungry! I'm going to make us all a snack," said Mr. Rounds.

What would they eat? They couldn't make popcorn in the microwave or toast in the toaster.

"What did you make, Dad?" asked Ben. Mr. Rounds was carrying a tray with peanut butter, crackers, and grapes from the fruit bowl.

CHAPTER 3
A Wonderful Night

While eating the snack, Ben hopped up from the couch. "Music!" he shouted. "How did we forget music? Let's play a song!" Ben ran and grabbed his guitar and Courtney got her flute. "You can play this tambourine, Josh," said Ben.

Everybody gathered around as Mr. Rounds took his seat at the piano. "Let's sing some old favorites that we all know by heart," said Mrs. Rounds. "That way I won't have to hold up a candle for Dad to see the music!"

"Well, it's certainly getting late," Mr. Rounds said an hour later.

"I had no idea I could have so much fun without using electricity!" Courtney said.

"I know," Ben replied. "There's still a lot more we could do, too, like playing cards or working on a puzzle."

Mom laughed. "We can do those other things whenever we want. It doesn't have to be Earth Day for us to unplug!"

"But right now it's time for me to walk Josh home," said Mr. Rounds.

"Thanks for all the fun," Josh said.

"Maybe we could plan an electricity-free night once a week. What do you guys think?" asked Mrs. Rounds.

"Definitely!" cried the kids.

Mr. Rounds grinned. "Then it's a plan!"

Respond to Reading

Summarize

Use important details to help you summarize *Family Night Unplugged.*

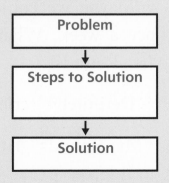

Text Evidence

1. How do you know *Family Night Unplugged* is fiction? GENRE

2. How is the problem of living without electricity solved? Tell the steps to the solution. PROBLEM AND SOLUTION

3. Use context clues to figure out the meaning of *knew* on page 11. HOMOPHONES

4. Write about another problem Ben solves at the end of the story. Tell what the problem is and how he solves it. WRITE ABOUT READING

Compare Texts

Find out how you can save electricity.

Tips for Saving Power

It is very easy to save electricity! Take a trip around your house. Are you using more electricity than you need? Check the living room and see if a computer, a television, or a radio is on. If you are not using these things, turn them off. How about lamps? If it is light outside or you are not using them, make certain the lamps are turned off, too.

Tetra Images/Alamy

The next stop is the bedroom. Are there any appliances running that should be turned off? Place your hand near the windows. Do you feel any air coming through? Make sure your windows are closed tightly. If air from outside can leak in or out, it can waste electricity when the heat or air-conditioning is on.

If you hold a piece of paper in front of your window sill and the paper flutters, that means air is leaking through.

ENERGY SAVING TIPS

	Turn off the lights when you leave a room.
	Turn off electronic machines when not in use.
	Keep windows and doors closed when the heat or air-conditioning is on.
	Turn the dryer off as soon as clothes are done drying.

The last stop is the kitchen. It is best not to keep the refrigerator door open for too long, so try to decide what you want before you open it. Also, ask a parent to check that the refrigerator door closes tightly. That helps save electricity, too.

? Make Connections

How can spending time "unplugged" help protect Earth? ESSENTIAL QUESTION

How else can we protect Earth? TEXT TO TEXT

Focus on Science

Purpose To find out ways to help the environment

What to Do

Step 1 ▶ With a partner, brainstorm how you can help the environment and save energy and Earth resources.

Step 2 ▶ Make a list of all the things you can do.

Step 3 ▶ Using your list, make a plan for how you can save energy and Earth resources at home and at school. Write out your plan and share it with your partner. Then create a poster showing at least two of your ideas.

Conclusion Take your list and poster home and share them with your family.